STAYING ALIVE!

ISBN 978-0-9569072-0-2

MTS

This race and this country
And this life produced me, he said.
I shall express myself as I am.

James Joyce
(Portrait of the Artist as a Young Man)

Along The Road

I walked a mile with Pleasure;
She chatted all the way;
But left me none the wiser
For all she had to say.

I walked a mile with Sorrow,
And ne'er a word said she;
But, oh! The things I learned from her,
When sorrow walked with me.

Robert Browning Hamilton

MAKE MINE A 99!

aster Monday. The dawn chorus roused us from a long hard winter. Outside the rising sun rolled its sparkling eggs through tiny gaps in our bedroom shutters. Spiders ran for cover. Love was in the air. The sweet music of what happens. I was suddenly released into a turmoil of tears. Brendan stayed close, his big hand on my tummy. My weeping never bothered him. He'd say, Women cry for their men and boys who can't cry for themselves. But not so this time. Not so this day. Today I was crying for myself.

For nearly three years I'd been bleeding from my back passage. Hadn't told Brendan. Hadn't told anyone. Hoped it'd go away. Wouldn't even think the word Cancer. I know God heals. I also know most people are healed in praying for themselves. I've seen countless healings over the years. But time was passing and I wasn't getting any better.

Brendan asked, What's wrong Love?

I'm not well.

Not well?

I've been going to the toilet a lot.

For how long?

A long time.

After our last missions trip Brendan had suffered from a bad bout of diarrhoea. He said, Since the Philippines?

Before that.

What? That's nearly six months ago! Angela, why didn't you tell me sooner?

I did tell you.

When?

At Christmas.

What'd you say?

I said I was tired.

Brendan smiled. He said, Angela, I think I'm much better at interpreting dreams than I am at understanding what you're trying to tell me.

You never listen to me.

He kept quiet and dressed. I remained in bed. Later, Mary and Hannah, two of our fourteen children came to visit. Mary is a surgeon, Hannah a midwife. Brendan talked with them. They persuaded me to go to the local Accident & Emergency unit. Brendan and Mary accompanied me. At the clinic Mary and I saw the doctor first. Then Mary waited outside while I was examined. Afterwards Mary and Brendan came back in for the verdict. The Indian doctor stared at Brendan. He said, You look very familiar. Don't I know you?

I don't think so.

I have definitely seen you before. He glanced at my medical notes. He said, Mr. McCauley you're local. I must have seen you in the town or somewhere. I'm sure and certain I recognise you. Absolutely.

Awkward seconds ticked by. He kept smiling at Brendan. I remember now, he beamed. You are the writer man with the big family. You have written books about India. In fact my mother-in-law from Kerala has your books on her bookshelf. He glanced at Mary. He said, Your dad is very famous you know!

We all laughed.

He said he'd found a mass on examination and would be referring me to a specialist.

Mary asked, Hard mass?

Not hard exactly. More firm like.

Mary looked at Brendan. We all knew a hard mass often means cancer. We linked arms as we walked to the car park. I wanted to curl up and cry. We drove in silence. Halfway home Brendan swung the car towards Ardglass. He said, Let's go for an ice cream. After all it's Easter Monday!

I'm from a farming background, the sixth child of ten kids. Dad and Mom worked hard. I'd told Brendan of an incident that occurred on another Easter Monday over fifty years ago. Often on Saturday night after a hard week's work Daddy would drive us to the nearby seaside town of Newcastle for an ice cream. I'd yell, Make mine a 99! It's still my favourite cone. Ice cream on my chin and crunchy chocolate between my teeth.

That long-ago Easter Monday was a warm day of sunshine. I so wanted to do something special. I hung around hoping Dad might holler, Okay, Let's go! Make mine a 99! But it never happened. There was just the endless round and rhythm of work. Milk the cows, mend the gate, start the tractor, feed the chickens. No happy ice cream on my chin.

As we parked at Ardglass harbour I felt thankful for my husband and children. Brendan was faithful and caring with an ability to make ordinary days special. Shann, Brendan, Nora, Aaron, Mary, Hannah, Ruth, John, Patrick, David, Jacob, Isaac, Abraham and Angela were our great children. Together we could face whatever lay ahead. I thought of Psalm 127;

> *Behold, children are a heritage from the Lord,*
> *The fruit of the womb is a reward.*
> *Like arrows in the hand of a warrior,*
> *So are the children of one's youth.*
> *Happy is the man who has his quiver full of them;*
> *They shall not be ashamed,*
> *When they contend with their enemies in the gate.*

Afterwards we drove twenty miles to Newcastle, Co. Down, to inform Hannah of the outcome. Our artist son John was there. He said earlier he'd read the familiar story in Daniel chapter three about how the King of Babylon commanded everyone to bow down and worship a golden statue otherwise they'd be thrown into a fiery furnace. Shadrach, Meshach, and Abednego refused. The king went buck mad and had them bound and thrown into the furnace. Then he was shocked to see one who looked like the Son of God walking around in the fire with the unbound men.

When the King called them out they were totally unharmed. Not even the smell of smoke on them. The only things burned were the ropes. The King praised the God of Israel and decreed anyone speaking against

Him would be executed. The King said, What other God can save in this way?

John said, Mom I believe you'll also pass through your fiery trail unharmed. In the end there won't even be the smell of cancer on you. I nodded. Over the years God has taken Brendan and me through many troubles and trials and we've never denied him. We wouldn't start now! I asked Brendan to phone each of our children and let them know my situation. Our eldest child Shann was particularly apprehensive. Being a nurse she knew just how awful cancer can be. Fear was in the air.

Two weeks later we drove to the colonoscopy appointment fearing the worst. You could've cut our sadness with a knife. I said, Tell me something beautiful. Something sweet. Brendan started singing,

> *Because He lives, I can face tomorrow.*
> *Because He lives, All fear is gone.*
> *Because I know He holds the future,*
> *And life is worth the living just because He lives.*

Sunlight came streaming through the window. He repeated it. We both sang,

> *Because He lives, I can face tomorrow.*
> *Because He lives, All fear is gone.*
> *Because I know He holds the future,*
> *And life is worth the living just because He lives.*

Hours later beneath the laden cherry blossoms at Lisburn's Lagan Valley Hospital we cuddled and cried deep sobs. The nurse who performed the procedure said there was malignant cancer in my colon. She mapped my future in strong words softly spoken. She said, Angela you've a long hard road ahead of you. She mentioned radiotherapy, chemotherapy and an operation. She explained I'd need a temporary colostomy, an external bag worn on my abdomen to collect my waste. It would need to be emptied several times a day. She also explained more scans would be needed to see whether the cancer had spread or not.

A week later we were back at the hospital. The cherry blossoms were all so suddenly gone. I had a CAT scan. After a week I was again back for an MRI scan. The night before this scan I'd a warning dream in which I was clamped onto a stretcher as my body was passed into a long tunnel. In the dream I knew I had to comply with the medic's advice and quieten' my spirit. I recalled this dream as I listened to the noisy clunk clicking of the scanner. I was then clamped onto a pallet as in my dream and my body passed into the machine's tunnel. I was so glad of this warning dream otherwise I'd have been even more traumatized.

Then another long wait for results. By now our extended family all knew I'd cancer. They were anxious to know whether it'd spread or not. Everyone wondered what the future might hold. Would I live to celebrate my 60th birthday and my 40th wedding anniversary in the coming year? Would I live to see my children's children as God had promised me? Would I live to see all my children graduate from university? See all my beautiful girls married? Hold their lovely babies in my arms?

Brendan wasn't anxious. He said, Angela, God won't let us down. Jesus came to destroy the works of the devil and he hasn't finished yet. He looked me full in the eyes and he quoted Psalm 18:17. He said, You shall not die but you shall live and you shall declare the works of the Lord.

I swallowed hard and the oxygen failed.

I wasn't so sure anymore.

A DREAMER OF DREAMS

Brendan is a dreamer of dreams. One time in India he'd a dream in which God told him to write a book for the Indian prayer warrior Mariamma and her husband Thampy. This book is called *India - One Act of Kindness*. Mariamma had been praying for thirteen years for God to send a writer. In the early days of their ministry there were prophecies spoken in the backwaters about a time when their hidden testimony would be told all over the world. When Brendan first met Thampy and Mariamma their sphere of influence had grown from them being two homeless street preachers to overseeing over five hundred churches. Now the figure is closer to three thousand.

India - One Act of Kindness is a testimony to the present day work of Jesus Christ. Less than 3% of

India is Christian. India has 1.3 billion people and 300,000,000 gods. Yet the testimony of Jesus will always defeat the work of Satan. Revelation 12:11 says, And they overcame him by the blood of the Lamb, and by the word of their testimony; and they loved not their lives unto the death.

Brendan is a prophet. His life is dedicated to the testimony of Jesus Christ. Revelation 19:12 says, The testimony of Jesus is the spirit of prophecy. Part of Brendan's ministry is to give a voice to God's people. That book raised credibility, visibility and finance for God's work in India. More importantly it encouraged Christians worldwide as it gave testimony to what Jesus is doing today. Yet as an intercessor I knew there'd be a price to pay. I knew Satan would counterattack us. It's been a costly experience in all sorts of ways. Spiritual pressure. Financial pressure. Time pressure. Misunderstanding. Our vehicles were regularly damaged and destroyed in our own driveway. Our enemies knew where we lived.

I felt the constant need for prayer cover. Ideally I'd have liked a team of intercessors around me but it wasn't to be. God has always protected our family while Brendan has travelled. But after he wrote *India – One Act of Kindness* I became fearful. I started a Sunday afternoon meeting in the local parish hall. Brendan didn't believe God had called us to this yet he occasionally supported me. The only day we ever filled the place was a day when Brendan brought along a community of Indian people who were celebrating the birth of a baby. But in the end it became obvious Brendan was right. Some of our children came under attack. At this point I realised I'd been wilful. I thought I knew better but in the end I saw the error of my ways.

Then Brendan wrote another book for Mariamma called *Better Than Weapons Of War.* About her deliverance ministry. It's been published in various countries and translated into other languages. But from my perspective it's a case of the same old, same old. Spiritual pressure. Financial pressure. Time pressure. Much misunderstanding. It's been a costly experience. Our vehicles were regularly damaged and destroyed in our own driveway. Our enemies still knew where we lived.

At the same time my sons were all sprouting up. Once upon a time they were healthy young trout full of life and appetite constantly swimming around our feet. Now they were tall trees looking down on me. The last seven of our children are six strapping boys in a row and a beautiful girl called Angela. They're all taller than me. All think they know more than me. Brendan calls it *The Individuation Process*, the act of becoming a self. I call it towering over me. I feel their resistance and I don't like it. Now that I'm older I don't have the strength to make them do what I want. They'll do what Brendan says but I think he's way too easy on them. Oh for the days when they were all washed, teeth brushed, prayers said and in bed at 7 o'clock.

Genesis 3:16 says, I will greatly increase your pains in childbearing. I believe this pain not only refers to the short-term pain of childbearing but also to the lifelong pain of childrearing. Bit like Simeon's prophecy to Mary in Luke 2:35, And a sword will pierce your own soul too. Rearing children has a pain that only the mother knows.

Things were not easy. I was discouraged at not seeing fruit in some of my children's lives. Without faith it's all too easy to work oneself into an emotional frenzy that drains one of all strength and hope. At the beginning of the year God spoke to Brendan and me from 1 Kings 20 concerning Ahab the king of Israel and Ben-Hadad the king of Syria. Ben-Hadad is a type of Antichrist who assembles kings and countries against Israel. He's also like Antichrist in his totalitarian claims. He wants it all. The scripture says,

> *He sent messengers into the city to Ahab king of Israel, saying, This is what Ben-Hadad says: Your silver and gold are mine, and the best of your wives and children are mine.*
>
> *The king of Israel answered, Just as you say, my lord the king. I and all I have are yours.*
>
> *The messengers came again and said, This is what Ben-Hadad says: I sent to demand your silver and gold, your wives and your*

children. But about this time tomorrow I am going to send my officials to search your palace and the houses of your officials. They will seize everything you value and carry it away.

I felt this was a warning Satan was going to come after me, our children and our finances. I grew anxious. Brendan too felt it was a warning but he also thought it contained clear guidance for us not to compromise in any way whatsoever with the defeated Satan/Ben-Hadad spirit. As we read further we discovered that through listening to God's prophets Israel's army twice defeated Ben-Hadad. Yet instead of killing him, Ahab compromised and made a covenant with the defeated Ben-Hadad so that Ahab could set up markets to buy and sell in Damascus. Ahab's mistake was self-interest and not seeking guidance from God. Brendan said we would set our hearts to hear God's voice, obey his commands and hold fast to the testimony of Jesus.

Each morning Brendan would read the Bible to me and we'd pray. Each morning and night he'd also lay his hands on my back and proclaim healing. Before I was diagnosed Brendan had a dream about a fox in the bowels of a house. In the dream the fox knew Brendan was alerted to its presence. Its strategy was to keep perfectly still so as not to give its position away. In the dream Brendan realised he must persevere and drive the fox out from under the house. He knew the fox must not be allowed to remain. After my first encounter with the Indian doctor from A&E Brendan interpreted the house as being me and the fox in the bowels of the house as being the cancer in my bowel. From then on he constantly prayed against the fox, commanding it to leave my body in the name of Jesus.

Yet I was feeling more and more discouraged. Our children all excelled at school. All passed the 11-plus exam. All won places in grammar schools. The Belfast Telegraph ran a front-page story to highlight their achievement. They've gone to the best universities - Oxford, Cambridge, LSE London, Liverpool, Aberdeen, Glasgow, Edinburgh, Dundee, Trinity Dublin, Queen's and the University of Ulster. But I was feeling neglected. I was maintaining our home and praying for our family but it felt like an endless and thankless task. Brendan was getting on with his own work, preaching, praying, prophesying dreaming, writing and travelling. He's been to over sixty nations and although I've been to a couple of dozen of nations with him I still felt like I was going nowhere. It seemed my family were doing their own thing and I was left behind. I was losing perspective. My bleeding started around this time.

At the end of 2009 I heard a Jewish lady predict many unfulfilled personal prophecies would come to pass in 2010. I was reminded of a day almost thirty years previously on Sunday 24th May 1981 when Brendan and I were given our first prophetic word, at a time when like most people in our generation, we hadn't a clue God was still speaking to his children through prophecy. That word said,

My son you have come to my kingdom by many strange and diverse roads. You have known great pain and great unrest in your life. I am now unravelling your life. It will take more time but already you see my hand of blessing on you. Don't just look at the present and what you still desire in your life and marriage. You see the present but I see the end.

I want you to remember these words and feed upon them in your heart. Your end is to be in total unity in your home. Your end is to be in great blessing. Your end is for your wife to be a fruitful vine at your side and for your children to be raised up as olive shoots around your table. I see this end my son. You will not always be receiving ministry. There will come an end to this. There will come a time when you are both healed and your lives are totally unravelled.

You have both known great conflict in your relationship. But these last two years this conflict has been me working with you in order to unravel your lives. And I will continue to unravel your lives. I will continue to unravel the strange roads you have been down. But there will come an end to this unravelling. There will be an arriving at a place of health and healing.

At a place of freedom. At a place of blessing, where your home and your marriage and your children will be an example to all the flock. I see this end.

As you go through these coming weeks and months feed upon this word in your hearts. Never lose it. Lay hold of this word for it is my word to you. Know I will never leave you nor forsake you, no matter how sluggish you find yourself at responding to my teaching, no matter how weak you feel and no matter how stubborn you are in your hearts against my discipline. I assure you I will not faint nor grow discouraged with you for I have set my heart and my face towards you in order to see you through and to unravel your lives.

Both your hearts desire this. Both your hearts long to be free in my kingdom. You often express this yearning in different ways and say different things to one another. Often you cannot understand each other. Often you do not recognize the same hunger in both your hearts. Yet I tell you it is there and I tell you that I will bring you to a place of unity. Unity in worship. Unity in prayer. Unity in living in the practical issues of day-to-day life. I will bring you to unity in the faith says the Lord.

I can still see Brendan and me holding hands and sobbing. That word so resonated with us. Went to the very core of our being. Our lives did need unravelling. Unravelling from occult influences. Unravelling from superstition, traditional religion, atheism, conflict and riotous living. I smiled as I recalled the sentence, As you go through these coming weeks and months feed upon this word in your hearts. In those days I didn't understand much about prophetic language and prophetic timeframes. I assumed weeks and months literally meant weeks and months not realising as it says in 2 Peter 3,

> *But do not forget this one thing, dear friends: With the Lord a day is like a thousand years, and a thousand years are like a day. The Lord is not slow in keeping his promise, as some understand slowness. He is patient with you, not wanting anyone to perish, but everyone to come to repentance.*

Weeks and months turned into years. Much water would flow under the bridge before I'd finally give birth to all fourteen olive shoots around our table. And still the unravelling would go on. Still the unity would come. Still more freedom. More health. More healing. And we'd often be weak, stubborn, and sluggish. Often an enigma to one another. But God true to his word never did grow discouraged. He kept unravelling our lives one thorny issue at a time.

Yet I longed for more. I grew impatient. I wanted all of that prophetic word to come to pass and the sooner the better. There are over 3,000 promises in the Bible. Most of them are conditional on our response of faith and obedience. Without faith it's impossible to please God. But if we meet the conditions God is faithful to fulfil his promise to us. Similarly when we are given a prophecy how we respond to that word depends on whether or not it is fulfilled in our lifetime. Isaiah 55 says,

> *For my thoughts are not your thoughts,*
> *neither are your ways my ways,*
> *declares the Lord.*
> *As the heavens are higher than the earth,*
> *so are my ways higher than your ways*
> *and my thoughts than your thoughts.*
> *As the rain and the snow*
> *come down from heaven,*
> *and do not return to it*
> *without watering the earth*
> *and making it bud and flourish,*
> *so that it yields seed for the sower and*
> *bread for the eater,*
> *so is my word that goes out from my*
> *mouth:*
> *It will not return to me empty,*
> *but will accomplish what I desire*
> *and achieve the purpose for which I sent*
> *it.*

Prophetic words are spiritual seeds from the mouth of God. They must be planted in good ground and constantly watered otherwise they can so easily perish. All prophetic words go through the same process as the written word of God in our lives. This is the method mentioned by Jesus in the *Parable of the Sower*. God has given us all free will and will never override our choices. The wayside soil describes those who don't believe the word in the first place. Satan can easily snatch away a prophecy from such people. Like candy from a baby.

The rock represents those who are initially excited about the prophecy but because they're not grounded in God's love the word can't take root. When temptation and warfare come they give up too easily. They won't pay the price.

The thorns are those who are caught up in consumerism, the pride of life, the lust of the flesh and the lust of the eyes. The girls, the guys, the gold and the glory. The cares and riches of this world stop them being productive in the kingdom of God.

The good ground represents those who hear the word and keep it hidden in their hearts. They believe the word and regularly water it with prayer. Their prophetic words will move them forward into their destiny in order to fulfil God's end-time purposes for the earth. They also constantly fight against Satan and his demons from stealing their prophetic destiny. St Paul counsels Timothy about this warfare in 1 Timothy 1,

This charge I commit to you, son Timothy, according to the prophecies which went before on you, that you by them might war a good warfare; Holding faith, and a good conscience; which some having put away concerning faith have made shipwreck.

Paul says it's possible to lose our prophetic words and God's purposes for our lives. I didn't want any of my family to miss God's best. Perhaps I was being too eager. Certainly I was expecting high standards. I was regularly praying for the prophetic fulfilment that all my children would follow the Lord. But when I saw them doing their own thing and being wilful I became sad.

I read from Proverbs 15:30, A cheerful look brings joy to the heart, and good news gives health to the bones. On the other hand Proverbs 17:25 says, A foolish son brings grief to his father and bitterness to the one who bore him. Some of my children were being foolish. Proverbs 13:12 says, Hope deferred makes the heart sick, but a longing fulfilled is a tree of life.

We'd been given that prophetic word almost thirty years earlier. God had said he'd bring Brendan and me to unity in our marriage, in faith, in worship, in prayer and in working out everyday matters. To my mind these things were not coming to pass. Brendan for his part thought we were doing amazingly well. He believed God was really blessing us. But for me things were getting worse. The bleeding continued. At times I felt great disunity between Brendan and me. When I was upset and angry he'd just walk out of the room. He said he didn't want to quarrel. For my part I wanted to vent my frustration somewhere. Although I never mentioned my bleeding I still wanted him to fix things for me. I couldn't see a way forward. I was beginning to lose hope. I felt worn down and worn out.

I'd lost all interest in cooking and shopping. Lost all heart for homemaking. I daily felt I was losing my life.

THE SECRET OF RIOTS

At Christmas I'd lost all grace for meeting with people. I was also disheartened by the moral deterioration amongst many of my peers. Some who'd held responsible positions of authority in the community were now living like love struck teenagers. When I was a love struck teenager I thought like a love struck teenager and acted like a love struck teenager but now I've become a grandmother I've put away teenage ways.

I find it hard to know how to deal with the whole issue of vanishing values. The Irish society of my youth was founded upon Christian truth. Now we live like pagans. The Land of Saints and Scholars is no longer a safe place to talk about God's standards or moral absolutes without being viewed as a religious bigot. Affluence and pleasure is the order of the day. Abortion allowed. Marriage no longer sacred. Am I supposed to party with peers who are openly living in sin without saying a word? Whatever happened to us being the light of the world? Am I to forget all I learned in my youth? Was Dad and Mom's morality wrong? I think of Isaiah 59:

So justice is driven back,
and righteousness stands at a distance;
truth has stumbled in the streets,
honesty cannot enter.
Truth is nowhere to be found,
and whoever shuns evil becomes a prey.

In John 10:10 Jesus warns, The thief comes only to steal and kill and destroy; I have come that they may have life, and have it to the full. Satan goes after the weakest link. Much like a lion picking off the vulnerable of the herd. One of our girls required rescuing from London. She'd been working hard and playing hard. She became desperately sick with a bad form of transverse myelitis that could have left her permanently disabled.

Mariamma happened to be visiting. She and I went to London and prayed for this daughter who received deliverance. We brought her home and after much love and prayer she eventually got back on her feet. Now she is working in Uganda as a midwife on the mission fields.

Some of our boys lost focus. This showed in their academic work. One son failed half a module by a couple of marks. His prestigious university played hardball and made him resit all six exams. Brendan tried to motivate this child over the summer. He accompanied him to London for the week of exams. But another exam was missed by a few marks and he had to take a year out. He was a bright boy caught playing the fool. The University of Hard Knocks for him.

Brendan had a dream concerning another son. In the dream Brendan saw a black woman speaking in tongues. As the heavenly language left her lips it was translated into English. The interpretation said we needed to rescue this boy. So we contacted him and he came home. He definitely needed rescuing. He'd also failed at university, was taking a year out and was not telling us. He was concealing other things as well. I was disappointed. Later when Brendan and I were speaking at a church in Calgary, Canada we actually met this black lady from Brendan's dream.

Brendan and I have laid down our lives for our family. Laboured long and hard in our garden of children. We certainly don't want them or their offspring going to hell. Another son required three A's to do medicine. He missed one exam by a few marks. He also took a year out. I was discouraged with their lack of progress. Brendan looked for the silver lining. He quoted Proverbs 22;6, Train up a child in the way he should go, And when he is old he will not depart from it.

He tried romance. He took me to Paris but the joy never really kicked in. I loved seeing the sparkling lights on the Eiffel Tower. Enjoyed a good meal on the Champs Elysées but just didn't have the appetite for romance. Since Brendan wrote those books for India there's been constant pressure from the enemy. We've had to stay close to God. Every morning Brendan and I prayed and read the Bible as usual. That gave me strength for the day.

Around this time my prayer life suffered a setback. Each week I prayed with a few women. One of my favourite verses is from Matthew 18:20 where Jesus says, For where two or three are gathered together in my name, there am I in the midst of them. I suggested to the women we avail ourselves of a special offer and take a break in a hotel. We could get to know one another. Perhaps pray for the city. That was my notion. Others had different expectations. Our unity would be tested. Two months before this hotel break and four months before my cancer disclosure a Canadian prophetess Cindy Skinner emailed Brendan a dream. She wrote,

> *I was praying for you and Angela in the night and I had a dream in the morning. In my dream I was in your home and heard the words there was faulty wiring in your home.*

I was in your home and the bedroom I was sleeping in had a large exposed cable shooting off sparks. I remember Angela being concerned for my safety because I was sleeping in this room near this large cable wire that was shooting sparks. So it was decided I'd move to the basement area.

I was very aware of the wiring problems and it seemed the problem was throughout the house. I remember Angela was quite concerned about the wiring in the home but you seemed distracted in a sense and not as concerned. I really felt this was a high priority and was also very concerned that the wiring could start a fire in your home.

After I moved to the basement area I remember meeting five or six women intercessors who were also in the basement. They were praying for you, Angela and the ministry. I recall they looked weary and not entirely focused. They seemed to be distracted on what they were called to do. In the dream I remember thinking they needed some encouragement and teaching on intercession.

Brendan was abstracted from properly interpreting this

warning dream. Often he has so many dreams from family, friends and others he just doesn't have the time to look in depth at them all. He mentioned the sparks possibly represented words that might ignite a fire of conflict that could destroy a family or ministry. He said the large exposed cable could represent a powerful spiritual person not properly covered or under authority. He said, Perhaps your prayer group are the weary unfocused intercessors. We left it at that. Big mistake!

In retrospect I now feel our women's group were probably the unfocused intercessors of Cindy's dream. We were definitively weary. I was bleeding and telling no one and another lady had lung cancer. We were ill prepared. Many sparks flew and the upshot was I never went back to the group. Ben-Haddad was waging war and I was losing ground. I felt crushed and overwhelmed.

Brendan helps people to interpret their dreams. Acts 2:17 says, In the last days, God says, I will pour out my Spirit on all people. Your sons and daughters will prophesy, your young men will see visions, your old men will dream dreams. Brendan says there is a Niagara Falls like pouring out of God's Spirit in these days in the whole area of dreams and visions. On all people. Young and old, male and female, Christian and non-Christian. Billions are experiencing God speaking through dreams and visions.

We have moved to where we now live through dreams. We've had fourteen children because of dreams and visions. Brendan has travelled to many countries and initiated many things through dreams and visions. Brendan has saved people's investments through a dream. Some of our children have passed exams through dreams. We have been warned and guided through dreams and visions. We could write another book. In fact Brendan is going to write a book called *The Secret of Riots* very soon. Brendan uses the simple formula called *The Secret of Riots©* when teaching on dreams and visions. He applies the acronym RIOTS where

R = Revelation
I = Interpretation
O = Operation
T = Timing
S = Success

In order to get the full benefit from a dream Brendan says we need to get the first four correct - the full revelation, the correct interpretation, how to put it into operation and the proper timing - then we will have great success. It's one thing to know a stock market crash is coming. It's another thing altogether to know exactly when it's coming and what to do about it. One thing to know a tsunami is coming. Another thing to know when and where and whether prayer can stop it or not.

Brendan claims only God can give the correct interpretation. He says we need to hold our revelation before God until he reveals the full interpretation. This can take minutes, sometimes years. Brendan is very careful about these things but often in my intercessory eagerness I rush into getting a quick understanding. This happened when I was with the women at the hotel. The first night I'd a dream in which I saw the insides of a person. Another person I couldn't see was helping me search for something as we scooped out the insides of the first person. Eventually we found a pink crab in the first person's bowels.

I knew the pink crab represented cancer. The Latin meaning for cancer is crab and the Greek word karkinoma used by Hippocrates concerning cancer also means crab. The next morning I shared this dream with the women. We then all prayed for a lady in our group who'd lung cancer. Months afterwards when I shared this dream with Brendan he asked where exactly the crab/cancer was in the person in the dream.

I said, In the bowel.

And where was it in the lady you prayed for?

In the lung?

And where was it in you?

I said, In my bowel. So God was showing me I'd bowel cancer?

Looks like it.

The second night I was with the women at the hotel I'd another dream. In this dream I saw a badly beaten up red car. I felt the car represented me. After the weekend I really felt like that wrecked car. Brendan said he thought the red car dream was a God dream warning me about what Satan desired to do with my life and ministry. He said I should totally reject the dream and pray against it ever happening. I remembered when after I'd my eleventh child an Indian doctor said to me, Mrs McCauley your body is like a car. It will break down if you keep having more children. I disregarded him and went on to have three more children. Now Satan was bringing that image up again to discourage me and it was working. Physically and spiritually I felt like a wreck.

Yet it wasn't all doom and gloom. In springtime two brilliant rays of sunshine burst through my dark clouds in the form of two beautiful granddaughters. Stella was born to Brendan and Tamara in February looking just like her mom. Eilish was born in March to Aaron and Marta in difficult circumstances. I'd just visited our son Patrick in Glasgow. He'd been diagnosed with a very serious leg infection requiring a surgical operation. He seemed in good heart. Saying things like, I'm fine Mom. Everything's all right.

Our doctor daughter Mary was aghast. She said, Foolish boy. He didn't realise the seriousness of it all. People have died from that particular infection. When I arrived back from seeing Patrick my daughter Nora told me about Marta and Eilish's life-threatening situation. Marta's temperature had suddenly gone sky high and Eilish became distressed. Marta was immediately given a crash Caesarean section under general anaesthetic. They were traumatised.

Nora said she'd a dream the previous night in which I died. She was upset. I was upset. These attacks were wearing me down. Brendan saw the bigger picture. He said, Perhaps dying is Satan's plan for you. In that case we'll pray against it. Perhaps the dream means you are dying to self in some area and becoming more alive to Christ. In that case we'll pray for it. Angela don't jump to conclusions. Satan may have attacked Aaron and Marta but wait and see. God will work it together for good. Let's pray blessing on them.

He was right. Within the year a 23-year-old prophecy from the American prophet John Paul Jackson for Aaron kicked into glorious life. In 1987 John Paul prophesied one day Aaron and Brendan would travel together in ministry. What he didn't reveal was that Aaron's beautiful Slovakian wife Marta and their two children Sara-Joye and Eilish would also accompany them. Nor did he mention that I and our twelfth child Isaac would also come along. Three generations of McCauleys on the move in a cold and snowy land.

Aaron and Marta had been distributing children's clothes in needy areas of Slovakia when they encountered a community of Charismatic Catholics who were keen on having a Prophetic Conference. After one dream in which Pope Benedict XVI commissioned Brendan to minister to Catholics worldwide we were off and running. We held a prophetic conference for leaders and priests from the four corners of Slovakia. We also ministered to the leaders and members of three other Charismatic communities. In the end we couldn't cope with the open doors. One leader said he'd been waiting for ten years for something like this. Another said he'd dreamed about our coming three years previously.

Perhaps Satan somehow saw the potential spiritual breakthrough in Slovakia and tried to stop it by killing Marta and Eilish. I don't know. But I do know they did not die but they lived and they are proclaiming the works of the Lord. Many dreams were interpreted in Slovakia but one simple dream still haunts me. At the end of the conference two young leaders asked Brendan to interpret a dream involving them and a bear. In the dream they were in a forest. They saw a bear coming. They climbed to the top of a tall tree where they hoped they'd be safe. Suddenly the two-year-old daughter of one of the men toddled into the dream. The bear instantly tore her apart and devoured her right before their eyes. End of dream.

Brendan's interpretation was along the lines that we can't

fight

run away from spiritual warfare in the hope of keeping ourselves safe. Like King David we must learn to kill the lion and the bear that would attack the sheep in our care. We must fight for our children and our children's children. The young leader said he felt sick as he watched the bear devour his lovely daughter.

I thought of Nehemiah 4:14,

> *Don't be afraid of them. Remember the Lord, who is great and awesome, and fight for your brothers, your sons and your daughters, your wives and your homes.*

It's a sad truth that many of the children and grandchildren of parents involved in the Charismatic movement are now being devoured by Satan's brutal bears. Ferocious bears of secular humanism, individualism and unbelief. Unless they clearly learn to hear and obey God's voice they are no match for these deadly destroyers. We really must fight for our children and our children's children.

We must equip them to hear and obey God's voice. Enable them to interpret their dreams and visions and live a life that counts.

THE PRINCE OF GREECE

Fear constantly attacked me but Brendan was a bold as a lion. He quoted from 1 Corinthians 15:19, If only for this life we have hope in Christ, we are to be pitied more than all men. He also quoted from Philippians 1:21, For us, living means living for Christ, and dying is even better. He said, In every generation everybody dies. Nobody gets out of here alive. What we believe and how we live will be tested. But it's not just about us. It's also about the generations after us. The important thing is that we do God's will. Angela let's live well and die well. Let's finish our race in style.

Before he knew of my bleeding Brendan had booked a cheap ten-day-holiday to the Greek island of Zakynthos. We've been there many times. We know and love two prophetesses from there, Roby and Sister

Miriam. The holiday was scheduled a week after the scans just when the results were due. I was fearful of leaving home, a hedgehog curled up against an uncertain world. Had the cancer spread? How long might I live? Brendan on the other hand was determined to go. He said it'd give us a chance to build up my faith for healing. He boldly proclaimed, You shall not die but you shall live and you shall proclaim the works of the Lord.

I still wasn't convinced. I couldn't say that.

Then Brendan had a dream in which we were to travel somewhere. In the dream I kept walking on a few yards ahead of him. To our left was a long barbed wire fence. Brendan noticed some young New Age people behind this fence grouped around a small spring of water. There were other fences surrounding them. As he glanced at them he heard the word, Illegal. He sensed the New Age folk were trying to slake their spiritual thirst in an illicit way.

Then suddenly in the dream I came running back terrified. I pointed further along the fence to a place where a huge tiger was standing with its head towering over the fence. It was looking directly at us.

I screamed, Run! We must run!

Brendan stayed calm. He said, No! We won't run. We'll continue on our way. Don't fear that tiger. He can't get beyond the fence otherwise we'd all be dead.

In the dream I gripped Brendan's right hand as we walked onwards. When we came abreast of the tiger we suddenly entered into a hotel room at which point Brendan took off a long pale green mantle and hung it up on a brass hook right in the middle of the foyer. Then we walked upstairs, showered and put on new clothes for an event in the upper levels of the hotel. End of dream.

Brendan felt part of the dream's interpretation was we shouldn't give way to fear but we should continue with our holiday as scheduled. I wasn't so sure. I needed a sign. This was Saturday. We were due to travel on Monday.

A previously planned trip to Geneva to see our daughter Ruth and her husband, Stuart, hadn't worked out. An Icelandic ash cloud had grounded the flight. I was disappointed. But now the reality of cancer had knocked the heart out of me for travel. Brendan on the other hand was looking forward to the holiday. He knew I always flourished in sunshine. Also ours was to be a self-catering holiday. In my current condition I didn't feel up to making food. But like in his *Tiger Dream* Brendan was not for turning back.

In my heart of hearts I desired Mariamma Thampy to come from India and pray for me. We had helped India. Perhaps India could now help us again? I shared this with Brendan.

I said, I'd like Mariamma to come and pray with me.

Brendan grimaced. He said, Angela, India is a long way off. Mariamma can't just get a visa to travel whenever she wants. The system is very difficult in India. Often it's refusal after refusal as regards visas. Mariamma's a busy woman. Travel from India is expensive.

I said, Let's pray about it.

More grimacing.

I stayed in bed. In the afternoon Brendan came in from the garden. His hands were muddy. Suddenly his mobile played music. He fished it out from his parka. It was Mariamma. God's fingerprints on our life. Brendan's fingerprints on his jacket.

She said, Hello Brother Brendan, I'm in London to receive an award at Hillsong's *Colour Your World Women's Conference* in the Royal Albert Hall. But all the time, I hear the Lord telling me to ring Brendan and Angela. Ring them! Ring them! Ring them! So what's happening Brother Brendan? Is there a problem?

Brendan said, Mariamma. You're sucking diesel. Angela has cancer. Perhaps we can meet up in London on Monday.

Sure, said Mariamma. Please arrange it.

We were due to fly into London at 8 pm Monday evening and fly on to Zakynthos eleven hours later at 7am.

Brendan tried to arrange that Mariamma and her daughters Bini and Beena could travel from their hotel in Kensington to our place near Gatwick but it just wouldn't work out. It was near midnight on Sunday and Brendan still couldn't solve this riddle. Then the Lord dropped it into his spirit we should buy new flights so as to be in London early next morning and have plenty of time to spend with Mariamma.

Brendan said, Why didn't I think of that?

Because you're afraid to spend the money.

Thanks Love!

I was so strengthened by this quick answer to my prayer that I agreed to travel and wait until our return to discover just how bad the cancer was. I was very happy. So we changed to an earlier flight, travelled to Mariamma's hotel and went upstairs to her room where true to form she was casting out demons and breaking curses over people.

Brendan said, Looks a bit like my tiger dream.

Mariamma welcomed us and prayed for me. She looked me full in the face. She said, Angela I don't believe this sickness is unto death. It's not your time yet.

That night we discovered had we not changed our flight times we'd have completely missed our holiday because our original later flight was cancelled because of another Icelandic ash cloud. There was more to come. When we arrived in Zakynthos a cheery young rep asked the name of our hotel. When we told her she said, Oh sorry! There's been a problem. Please wait here. She went to talk with her supervisor. Brendan and I exchanged glances.

The supervisor apologised. She said, I'm so sorry but your hotel hasn't opened yet. Greece is in bad financial trouble at the moment. But fear not! We've decided to upgrade you to a much better hotel. All free of charge. Is that okay?

We nodded.

And better still we've also decided to upgrade you to an all inclusive basis which means all your food and drinks will be completely free of charge. Is that all right?

Brendan smiled. Somewhere far away a tiger groaned.

She asked, Any questions?

I said, Any chance of a king-sized bed?

She smiled, Why not?

In the end it worked out great. Our upgrade hotel was the perfect place for me. I was so encouraged by God shutting the mouth of the tiger, bringing Mariamma along and improving our hotel. It had two swimming pools, a lively one at the back and a quiet one at the front where we sunbathed. We were also greatly strengthened by our fellowship with Roby and Sister Miriam. This was an ideal situation for me. God had led us beside still waters to restore our souls. He had prepared a place for us in the presence of our enemies. I didn't have to cook a thing. Don't get no better!

Brendan prayed with me throughout the day as well as our daily routine of prayer and Bible reading. He also quoted healing scriptures and had me repeat them after him. He was doing all he could to build up my faith. One day he said, Angela I've being thinking about the incident with the Indian doctor at A&E on the day you first told me you were bleeding. Perhaps that was Jesus' way of showing us he was with us in the fiery furnace. Psalm 41:1 says, Blessed is the man that considers the poor: the Lord will deliver him in the evil day.

Brendan's interpretation resonated with me. One of my favourite scriptures, Hebrews 6:10 says, God is not unjust; he will not forget your work and the love you have shown him as you have helped his people and continue to help them. These thoughts warmed my heart. For many years Brendan and I have constantly considered the poor and needy. Continually Brendan had shunned the limelight so he could concentrate his energies into the needy third world.

Yes, I whispered, God will deliver us in our day of trouble. Nevertheless I knew a battle lay ahead.

Cancer - The Big C - can certainly take the wind out of one's sails. But Brendan kept saying, Cancer is only a name - a name far below the name of Jesus and thankfully Jesus is still healing the sick and still destroying the works of Satan.

We met our friend Roby a number of times. We prayed and interpreted dreams. We took a ferry to visit Sister Miriam who was staying with a teacher and his family on the mainland. As usual Miriam was fussing and sweating in her long black habit as she cooked the fish, pork and chicken. Like being back in Bible times - sunshine, laughter, olives, bread and wine.

The teacher, Dionysus, is also an organic gardener. How sweet his fruit and vegetables. He drove us to his nearby orange grove and plucked a box of fresh oranges to squeeze juice for us. Later when I'd learn my tumour was the size of an orange I'd think back to this day. They were sweet thick-skinned oranges like those of my youth. Dionysus was sad and a little angry because the supermarkets had declined his entire orange harvest because they were a little too big for their liking. A whole grove of perfect oranges left hanging to rot on the trees

Dionysus and his daughter played Greek music and Brendan sang and recited Irish poetry. Sister Miriam sang Psalms. The talk turned to prophecy. Brendan quoting the Scriptures said prophecy was easy. It was a gift from God. Dionysus was not convinced. He thought one had to go about in sack cloth and ashes and live forty years in a cave in order to be able to prophesy.

Either that or have fourteen children, joked Brendan.

Next day Dionysus and his wife drove us to the ancient site of Olympia, a religious centre with numerous temples dedicated to Zeus the father of the Greek gods. It's also the original site of The Olympic Games. These games from before 776 BC were instituted to honour Zeus. Our modern Olympic torch still symbolizes the pagan fire imparted by the god Prometheus. As we strolled through this pagan place I thought of the story from Daniel 10, which gives us a behind-the-scenes glimpse of the invisible war in the heavenly realm. For three weeks Daniel had been fasting and mourning over captive Israel; then an angel arrived. He said,

> *Do not be afraid, Daniel. Since the first day that you set your mind to gain understanding and to humble yourself before your God, your words were heard, and I have come in response to them. But the prince of the Persian kingdom resisted me twenty-one days. Then Michael, one of the chief princes, came to help me, because I was detained there with the king of Persia. Now I have come to explain to you what will happen to your people in the future, for the vision concerns a time yet to come.*

War occurred in heaven because a prophetic person was willing to fast. Yet it required three weeks of struggle with a territorial strongman called the prince of the kingdom of Persia and the help of the archangel Michael before God's messenger could break through the second heaven with his message for Daniel concerning Israel in the latter days. The angel then told Daniel he had to return to fight with the prince of Persia - and afterwards the prince of Greece will come.

The prince of Persia is the invisible demonic strongman behind the force of Islam today. A force still committed to the complete destruction of Israel.The prince of Greece is the demonic strongman behind all the Greek philosophy that still controls most Western thought today, its pagan rationalism denying all forms of supernatural reality. Our Western Churches and educational systems are totally paralysed by this satanic worldview. Christians and Churches who deny the power of God's Holy Spirit's power have been hamstrung by this prince of Greece. Between them these two strongmen keep billions of people in spiritual darkness. They are the sworn enemies of Jesus Christ and his Church.

Brendan and I have seen this prince of Greece symbolism depicted in the architecture of government buildings in Belfast, Dublin, Edinburgh, Washington, Paris, London, Rome and a host of other cities. But the truth is this Greek spirit can never defeat the Persian spirit. No Western government based on Greek rationalism can ever defeat Islam. Only the restored church of Jesus Christ can do that.

As we walked amongst these old gods I was amazed that from such a small place dark forces were released that captured the minds of so much of the Western world. But then I recalled Daniel's interpretation of Nebuchadnezzar's Dream. In Daniel 2 the prophet explains,

> *While you were watching, a rock was cut out, but not by human hands. It struck the statue on its feet of iron and clay and smashed them. Then the iron, the clay, the bronze, the silver and the gold were broken to pieces at the same time and became like chaff on a threshing floor in the summer. The wind swept them away without leaving a trace. But the rock that struck the statue became a huge mountain and filled the whole earth.*

Then Daniel says,

> *In the time of those kings, the God of heaven will set up a kingdom that will never be destroyed, nor will it be left to another people. It will crush all those kingdoms and bring them to an end, but it will itself endure forever. This is the meaning of the vision of the rock cut out of a mountain, but not by human hands — a rock that broke the iron, the bronze, the clay,*

the silver and the gold to pieces. The great God has shown the king what will take place in the future. The dream is true and the interpretation is trustworthy.

As I stood on this pagan site with malignant cancer in my body I knew beyond all shadow of a doubt that Jesus Christ is the rock not cut by human hands. His kingdom is still growing into that huge mountain that will fill the whole earth. Fill it with the knowledge of the glory of God as the waters cover the sea. It is his kingdom and his kingdom only that will finally overcome the prince of Persia and the prince of Greece. I knew in my heart. It is his kingdom alone that can overcome the cancer in my body and extend my life. My body is the temple of the Holy Spirit and no foul spirit of cancer shall kill me before my time.

He must increase and cancer must decrease.

THE BODY OF CHRIST

n Northern Ireland we have physically and verbally murdered one another for centuries. Here Catholics and Protestants so easily and so quickly consign one another to hell. In John 13 Jesus says, My children, a new command I give you: Love one another. As I have loved you, so you must love one another. By this everyone will know that you are my disciples, if you love one another. In John 17 Jesus says,

> *My prayer is not for them alone. I pray also for those who will believe in me through their message, that all of them may be one, Father, just as you are in me and I am in you. May they also be in us so that the world may believe that you have*

sent me. I have given them the glory that you gave me, that they may be one as we are one - I in them and you in me — so that they may be brought to complete unity. Then the world will know that you sent me and have loved them even as you have loved me.

Jesus prayed we love each another just like he loves us. Then unbelievers will recognize us as his followers and they'll believe in him also. Jesus wants an observable unity. Viewing other Christians and their churches as enemies is ugly for non-Christians to watch. We should be warm and loving with other Christians. Humble enough to show an interest in what God is doing through them. If we are just as alienated and superficial in our relationships with each other as everyone else then no amount of empty rhetoric or slick marketing will ever make up for it! Nothing convinces unbelievers that God exists like the discovery of Christians who love one another.

Although I mentally understood all this I wasn't always great at putting it into practice. Unity is extremely hard work - contested at every turn by Satan. Sometimes I found myself at loggerheads with people. I'd often complain Brendan didn't love or understand me, my children didn't love or understand me, other Christians didn't love or understand me. I kept many Christians at arms length. Yet in my day of trouble God used all these people to love and heal me. God treated me to a practical outworking of the body of Christ. In

1 Corinthians 12, St Paul says,

> *Now the body is not made up of one part but of many. If the foot should say, "Because I am not a hand, I do not belong to the body," it would not for that reason cease to be part of the body. And if the ear should say, "Because I am not an eye, I do not belong to the body," it would not for that reason cease to be part of the body. If the whole body were an eye, where would the sense of hearing be? If the whole body were an ear, where would the sense of smell be? But in fact God has arranged the parts in the body, every one of them, just as he wanted them to be. If they were all one part, where would the body be? As it is, there are many parts, but one body.*
>
> *The eye cannot say to the hand, "I don't need you!" And the head cannot say to the feet, "I don't need you!" On the contrary, those parts of the body that seem to be weaker are indispensable, and the parts that we think are less honourable we treat with special honour. And the parts that are unpresentable are treated with special modesty, while our presentable parts need no special treatment. But God has combined the members of the body and has given greater honour to the parts that*

unity

lacked it, so that there should be no division in the body, but that its parts should have equal concern for each other. If one part suffers, every part suffers with it; if one part is honoured, every part rejoices with it.

Romans 16:20 says if we walk in unity and love then God will soon crush Satan beneath our feet. The moment I stopped hiding my bleeding from Brendan there was an immediate shift in the pressure. Some weight lifted. A stone rolled away. As if God kicked in and the body of Christ was enabled to work. And work it did! Catholics and Protestants. Irish and English. Christians I'd previously quarrelled with were moved to help me. Christ used his body to support me. Ephesians 4 says, Speaking the truth in love, we will in all things grow up into him who is the Head, that is, Christ. From him the whole body, joined and held together by every supporting ligament, grows and builds itself up in love, as each part does its work. I've read somewhere one horse can pull six tons while two horses can pull thirty-six tons. Sounds a bit like Ecclesiastes 4,

Two are better than one,
because they have a good return for their work:
If one falls down,
his friend can help him up.
But pity the man who falls
and has no one to help him up!
Also, if two lie down together, they will

keep warm.
But how can one keep warm alone?
Though one may be overpowered,
two can defend themselves.
A threefold cord is not quickly broken.

After Brendan told our family about my sickness some log-jam moved and love flowed freely. Our friends Mick and Jean Rodgers called in and prayed. The body of Christ was building itself up. That night I'd a dream about an eight-foot tall man with a dark suit and glowing orange eyes. He emerged from downstairs in our home. I knew he was a demon. He looked very similar to a demon of rejection I'd seen years earlier. My mother was also in the dream. I was scared. I began to shout, Mommy! Mommy! Mommy!

My shouting woke Brendan. He asked, What's wrong Love?

I told him my dream. He'd also been dreaming. In his dreams he was going about God's work but I kept cutting across him saying, Don't do this. Don't do that. I immediately prayed about these dreams and discerned the orange-eyed strongman was a generational spirit of rebellion that'd affected me all my life. Brendan prayed against this spirit and broke its power over me. I knew I was instantly delivered. This spirit had greatly troubled my life and my relationships. Many times my attitude has been way over the top in my response to people and situations because of rejection and rebellion. But thank God things were changing.

Next day I asked our friends Robert and Carol Cardwell to come to a meeting in our home and pray for me. Brendan had a prior appointment but would arrive later. Carol spoke from Genesis 15 and quoted God's promise to Abram of how he'd go to his ancestors in peace and be buried at a good old age. That witnessed with me. She also quoted,

> *Do not be afraid, Abram.*
> *I am your shield,*
> *your very great reward.*

In my spirit I could hear,

> *Do not be afraid, Angela.*
> *I am your shield,*
> *your very great reward.*

Robert has been nicknamed Shaking Robert because he shakes vigorously when the Holy Spirit comes upon him. He's often turns up at our home when we need encouragement. Brendan and I are always open to people of the Spirit. Robert has an unusual manifestation but as far as we've been concerned the fruit has been good. Robert prayed for our friend Rachel McDowell and she now has a growing ministry of intercession. He prayed for our son Aaron at one of Brendan's conferences and he literally shook Aaron into a new level of ministry.

Caroline Curtis came into our lives around this time. Caroline, a prophetic intrcessor, was a woman sent by God. She often strengthened and encouraged us all with her prayers and lovely meals. Sweet Caroline.

One day our daughters Hannah and Angela were praying with Rachel McDowell. I joined in. Rachel has a gift of seeing inner visions. She'd a vision of a worm in an apple for me. In the vision someone wanted to cut out perfectly good parts of the apple in order to get rid of the worm. Rachel sensed only the worm needed to be removed. She also felt the worm represented bitterness. Rachel knew little or nothing about my condition. She was unaware the usual procedure is to cut away the cancer along with some good parts of the colon. Rachel's vision was a perfect picture of my situation. Only the worm of cancer required removal.

Two days after my diagnosis I was praying with my friend Naomi Gadd. Naomi mentioned the English healing evangelist Melvin Banks was holding a meeting in Brendan's old hometown of Lurgan that very night. Twenty years previously Brendan had been healed of full body psoriasis when Melvin prayed for him. At the Lurgan meeting Melvin preached from Luke 8 about Jesus healing the woman with the issue of blood. He was reading my mail. Afterwards when he laid hands on me he looked into my eyes and said, You have great faith. God will make you whole.

Four days later an English Prophetess, Shirley Bowers came to visit. Shirley is leader and founder of *Arise*

Ministries, a group of Christians of mixed denominations dedicated to prayer, healing and reconciliation. She is also the author of *From History to Hope*, the story of how God has led her in a journey of repentance for the pain Oliver Cromwell had inflicted upon Ireland. I was deeply touched by this book. Shirley lives and fellowships in Huntingdon the birthplace of Oliver Cromwell. We live in an old house in Downpatrick that belonged to Cromwell's niece.

Shirley told us her story. She said Cromwell's hatred of Catholics was like a cancer spreading from Huntingdon across the land and into Ireland. She presented us with a letter of apology from the Huntingdon Churches. She then prayed for Brendan and I. God told her to specifically pray Brendan be given back his voice. What she didn't know was twenty years previously some English prophets had put a sticking plaster over Brendan's mouth and told him to keep quiet. She repented to Brendan for this act of the Empire Spirit. She said Ireland had been robbed of its true voice since Cromwell's time. She said, Brendan it's now your time to speak. She also prophesied whereas Cromwell destroyed Irish families Brendan and I would bring healing to Irish families.

There was a lovely young lady with Shirley called Isla Brown. Isla gave me a CD of healing verses from the Bible. That CD has been a big blessing. Although I've known and used most of those scriptures over the years it was great to have them all on one CD. Whenever I was tempted to doubt I was being healed

I'd listen to them and be encouraged. Faith comes by hearing and hearing by the word of God.

Shirley was a breath of fresh air. Ever since I became a committed believer I've also always prayed with Christians from other denominations. I've always known unity was in a top place on God's heart. I've always known we Christians in Northern Ireland needed to repent of our bitterness towards one another. 2 Chronicles 7:14 says,

> *If my people, which are called by my name, shall humble themselves, and pray, and seek my face, and turn from their wicked ways; then will I hear from heaven, and will forgive their sin, and will heal their land.*

After my diagnosis our daughter Hannah began to pray and fast for twenty-one days. Towards the end she saw a vision of a large white snake wrapped around our house in an attempt to crush the life out of us. In Hannah's dream a lady in a white blouse came and prayed against this snake. Hannah was made aware this lady had previously given us pictures.

When Brendan heard the dream, he said, Hannah this woman in your dream is our Dutch friend Nanda from Derry. She is a righteous prophetess signified by the white blouse. She has both given us physical pictures and spiritual pictures (visions and prophecies) over the years. That beautiful flower picture on our landing was painted by her. God is showing us that Nanda is the one to pray against this demonic snake and its assignment against us.

Without knowing anything about Hannah's dream Nanda rang and asked if she and her husband Gerrit could come to visit. I had a prior dental appointment so I was hesitant but Brendan said, Let them come. The time is right. So they came and prayed around our property. Seemed like the siege was lifted. Prior to Nanda and Gerrit praying we'd stopped holding regular meetings in our home. Afterwards Brendan restarted the meetings and the Holy Spirit flowed freely. Jackie McArthur from Bangor, Brendan's favourite prophetic minstrel, came often to our home in those days and led worship. Jackie's sister Helen is also battling cancer so he was very sympathetic. He prayed and prophesied into our lives and our children's lives. He was a great strength. He restored the banner of worship to us.

In February I read from Psalm 35,

> *Contend, O Lord, with those who contend with me;*
> *fight against those who fight against me.*
> *Take up shield and buckler;*
> *arise and come to my aid.*
> *Brandish spear and javelin*
> *against those who pursue me.*
> *Say to my soul,*
> *I am your salvation.*
> *May those who seek my life*
> *be disgraced and put to shame;*

may those who plot my ruin
be turned back in dismay.
May they be like chaff before the wind,
with the angel of the Lord driving them away;
may their path be dark and slippery,
with the angel of the Lord pursuing them.

Whenever I'd feel overwhelmed I'd envisage God's angels whipping my enemies up the Belfast Road far from us. One day a young prophet came to see us. He had two words from God for me. He spoke to Brendan first. Then Brendan allowed him to pray for me. I was touched by his compassion. The words he brought confirmed what God had already said. One was from Isaiah 62:4, No longer will they call you Deserted, or name your land Desolate. But you will be called Hephzibah, and your land Beulah; for the Lord will take delight in you, and your land will be married.

I'd been praying God would heal my land - the land of my marriage and the land of my family. Hephzibah and Beulah are Hebrew words. Hephzibah means my delight is in you. Beulah means married. The Lord was healing my feelings of disunity and isolation. He was saying he delighted in me. Saying I was part of his bride. Brendan and I were Beulah. He and God delighted in me. I was strengthened.

This prophet also had a vision of a large tree with a family of foxes in its roots. He quoted from Song of Solomon 2:15, Catch for us the foxes, the little foxes

little foxes

that ruin the vineyards, our vineyards that are in bloom. Another translation says, Catch all the foxes, those little foxes, before they ruin the vineyard of love, for the grapevines are blossoming!

Little foxes are mischievous and dangerous, like little sins of bitterness and rebellion that seem small but soon spread themselves and become fatal to individuals, families and churches spoiling all fruitfulness. This word reminded me of Brendan's dream about a fox hiding in the bowels of my house. This prophet who is also an artist came to see us twice. Second time he gave us an oil painting of lilies based on Jesus' teaching from Matthew 6,

> *Consider the lilies of the field, how they grow: they neither toil nor spin; and yet I say to you that even Solomon in all his glory was not arrayed like one of these. Now if God so clothes the grass of the field, which today is, and tomorrow is thrown into the oven, will He not much more clothe you, O you of little faith? Therefore do not worry, saying, What shall we eat? or What shall we drink? or What shall we wear? For after all these things the Gentiles seek. For your heavenly Father knows that you need all these things. But seek first the kingdom of God and His righteousness, and all these things shall be added to you. Therefore do not worry about tomorrow,*

for tomorrow will worry about its own things. Sufficient for the day is its own trouble.

I'd read somewhere lilies are a symbol of a completed work. I knew I'd be healed. God would finish his work. A couple of prophets, Stephen and Judy McGookin came to visit. Stephen has suffered from colon cancer, which left him on the verge of death in intensive care. We were encouraged by their fellowship. They helped me realise many others are also facing great trials and are still pressing on. Judy shared how she also suffered when her husband was sick.

At the beginning of my cancer God spoke to me from 1 Corinthians 12, If one member suffers, all suffer together; if one member is honoured, all rejoice together. We in the body of Christ share a very special oneness. When one suffers we all suffer. We should work together to build up and to defend one another. Stephen and Judy talked of people who supported and encouraged them. I knew it'd be the same with me.

Quietly without telling anyone our fifteen-year-old daughter Angela did a twenty-one day fast for my healing. She stayed with our eldest daughter Shann and her family for part of the time. Angela started teaching Shann's children how to speak in tongues and prophesy. She played worship songs for them. One of the songs had the voices of angels on it. Shann's kids were excited. Angela prayed for them to be baptised in the Holy Spirit and to speak in tongues. When

Shann's oldest girl, Shann Rois came to visit she said, Granny, guess what? I'm learning two new things this summer, speaking in tongues and doing ballet. Towards the end of her fast Angela had a vision of a fox leaving a house. I believed this meant the cancer would go.

All around me life continued as normal. Children studied hard and did exams. Birds built nests and hatched eggs in our hedges. Snowdrops and daffodils came and went to their own rhythms. Roses bloomed and smelt as sweet as ever. We didn't have the energy to garden much this year. I grow vegetables and Brendan grows flowers. He claims people starve quicker without beauty than food. Our dog Finn continued to need long walks. Beautiful grandchildren were born. Life's little problems needed daily solving. The kids, dog, cat and hens needed feeding. Bills needed paid. Logs chopped. Birthdays celebrated. Prayers said. Dreams dreamed.

The Scripture says that our children will stand with us against our enemies in the gate. And so it was. I'm thankful my husband and children were such a support in my time of trouble. Shann and Brendan, our oldest children, are married and living near Dublin. Each night they and their families faithfully prayed for Granny. I'm a great believer in the power of children's prayer. Psalm 8:2 says, From the lips of children and infants you have ordained praise because of your enemies, to silence the foe and the avenger.

A close friend of my daughter Nora died of cancer

during these days. Nora rallied round and organised the whole family to spring-clean our house when Brendan and I were in Zakynthos. Aaron, Marta and their kids visited us, cooked for us and prayed for us often. Mary, a busy surgeon, also fasted twenty-one days for me. She's a dreamer of dreams. Her dreams and prayers have strengthened and encouraged me. Hannah who works locally as a midwife was a constant backing all during my sickness. She'd call before work and on her days off to talk and pray. Shann, Mary and Hannah have all treated cancer patients. They knew what I faced.

Ruth who lived in Switzerland during this time flew home three times and was an enormous encouragement to Brendan and me. John entertained and cooked for us. Patrick and David at University texted and emailed often as did Jacob who was helping orphans in South Africa. Isaac prayed, dreamed and made soup. The home birds Abraham and Angela made early morning porridge and daily lifted my heart.

One day Brendan asked me to grade his support. He said, How well did I do on a scale of one to ten? I didn't have to think long. I said, On a scale of one to ten you went from minus 15 to plus 15. From frozen to sizzling.

He said, Praise God! Jesus said we should be either cold or hot so I was doing okay?

We visited a Christian fellowship in Belfast called *Coracle*. They're very prophetic people. The leaders

Terry and Geri offered to pray for me. Dreams and visions and prophecies abounded. One woman had a vision of a shield of protection all around the bottom half of my body. She knew nothing about my condition. Another girl had a vision of a cauliflower like appendage. My daughter Mary said that's what a cancer looks like. Another lady prophesied about a volcano erupting. Two men proclaimed God was going to smash the cancer.

Another young man shared a dream he believed was for me. In his dream he saw a stainless steel pipe that needed cleaning. The sense being there was no need to be anxious. It was a perfectly good stainless steel pipe. It just needed cleaned and God was going to do the cleaning by his Holy Spirit. I was comforted and strengthened by this dream. Six weeks later I received a confirmation of this prophetic dream through our good friend Harry Ferguson from Dundonald. Harry sent Brendan an email. It said,

> *We were praying for Angela at prayers after lunch yesterday with David and Di Harper from England and ministry friends of theirs Roy and Moira Waldrum from New Zealand. After prayers Roy felt the Lord had given him a vision of a clean exhaust pipe. And with the colon being the body's exhaust, he believed it would be well with Angela.*

Around this time my daughter Mary told me a story. She'd watched a documentary about a young woman who'd cancer. The doctor only gave her two years to live. This woman quit her job rented an apartment with a view and decided to enjoy herself as she awaited death. She bought a large screen television and watched funny videos and films. She lived off pizzas and takeaways. A couple of years later all her money was gone and she was still here. She went and asked the doctor when she might expect to die. The doctor examined her and found she was cancer free.

I laughed when I heard this story. I remembered how in the past when we owned a television occasionally Brendan would rent funny videos so as to cheer me up. Brendan claimed I was a very hard person to rent videos for. I wouldn't watch anything with sex, violence or bad language. He said that didn't leave a big choice. After hearing Mary's story I thought I'd like to watch some funny videos again. Problem was we didn't own a TV.

I told Brendan, I'd like him to buy a large screen television. He was not impressed. He reminded me it was my desire to rid our home of the television in the first place. He said, It's all too expensive just to satisfy a spur of the moment whim. I agreed with his logic. A couple of days later I received an email from our friend Hilary Ferguson. She said months previously someone had given her an old large screen television on a free to good home basis. Now Hilary was cleaning out her garage and I kept coming to her mind. Did I want a big screen TV? Hilary is the last person in the world Brendan would have expected to offer us a television. If it's from Hilary, said Brendan, it must be from God.

I was so encouraged God saw my desire and fulfilled it for me. My son Abraham set things up. Another friend loaned me some DVDs and we were in business. I laughed and cried my way through half a dozen movies before I thought, Oops? What am I doing? Why am I wasting my days watching these crazy movies? It's all fantasy.

Thus ended my short-lived career as a movie critic. Yet I was very affirmed by the whole thing. Very blessed. I felt by the provision of that television set God was showing his special care for me.

What a loving God we have.

A TSUNAMI OF SADNESS

arly morning a couple of days after our Greek holiday and a tsunami of sadness hit. The oxygen failed and the sun darkened. We hadn't received the results of the scan yet. Our children were anxious to know just how bad things really were. All morning doom clouds hovered. In the afternoon I picked up a copy of *The Divinity Code*, by Adrian Beale and Adam F Thompson. This is Brendan's favourite book on decoding dreams and visions. On their website Brendan has written, The Metaphor Dictionary alone is worth its weight in gold. The absolute best I have ever seen. If you had offered me $10,000 or this book, I'd have taken the book. It's that powerful. Brendan loves that book because it saves him loads of time when interpreting dreams.

I just happened to open to the page where it spoke about suicide. It said,

Suicide: (1) Warning of pending suicidal thoughts; (2) Oppression and/or depression; (3) Hopelessness; (4) Spirit of heaviness; (5) Self Hatred; (6) Wanting to give up; (7) Self Pity.

Definition one didn't seem to apply but the rest fitted like a glove. I'd lost vision. I thought Brendan disapproved of me. I wasn't happy with myself. Maybe he'd be better off without me. I was tired of mountains not moving, things not changing. I wanted unconditional love. But when I tried to express myself it all came out wrong. I know I sounded harsh and complaining but I couldn't stop it. Brendan said, Angela, it's hard to hug a hedgehog.

After reading those definitions I realised I was under attack. I'd become soft on whether I wanted to live or not. Heaven might be happier. Brendan sometimes says, If Satan couldn't put you into hell then the sooner he can get you to heaven the better. Then you won't be able to finish God's work. Ephesians 2:10 says, For we are God's workmanship, created in Christ Jesus to do good works, which God prepared in advance for us to do.

Often the real enemy of faith is not unbelief but memory. Negative memories keep us stuck in the past while faith has the power to open doors to the future. Hebrews 11:1 says, Now faith is the assurance that what we hope for will come about and the certainty that what we cannot see exists. One of Satan's strategies is to keep us focused on bad things in the past. Then he can sabotage our God-given hope. For some reason I remembered a dream I had over twenty years ago. In that dream I was being harassed by demons. At one point I said to the demons, I'm going to tell my husband about you. At that they squealed and ran away. I needed to remember Brendan was not my enemy.

The next day our son Isaac was discussing healing with some friends. A Christian youth leader joined in. In the past Mariamma had prayed for one of these friends and he'd received substantial healing. But the youth leader didn't believe in healing and the rest of the young Christians were being influenced by his unbelief including the boy who'd previously received healing. Isaac was dismayed by their scepticism. He shared this incident with Brendan when they were walking our wolfhound, Finn.

As young boy Isaac had suffered from a persistent glue ear problem that started affecting his learning. Eventually a surgical procedure was scheduled. On the morning of the operation Isaac woke up with the bottom part of his right hand covered in a gold-dust-like substance. He showed this to Brendan. Brendan had experience of this gold dust or Glory Dust phenomena in India, Sri Lanka and America. He'd met poor people who'd shown him mouths filled with what they claimed were supernatural gold teeth. He had gold dust and oil appear on his own hands and face at some of these meetings. He'd met people who were healed at these meetings. Brendan is not against signs and wonders. He well knows the Mark 16 passage where Jesus says,

> *And these signs will accompany those who believe: In my name they will drive out demons; they will speak in new tongues; they will pick up snakes with their hands; and when they drink deadly poison, it will not hurt them at all; they will place their hands on sick people, and they will get well.*

Most of our believing family speak in tongues; drive out demons and pray for the sick on a regular basis. We haven't literally picked up snakes yet but we know St. Paul once did in Acts 28. As regard poison, they sell it day and daily in Irish pubs but that's another story. When Brendan saw the gold dust on Isaac's hand he said, Isaac, looks like everything's going to be okay. He then prayed for healing in Jesus' name and promptly forgot all about it.

I took Isaac to the hospital and held his hand as he sat in a little blue gown swinging his feet. The doctor arrived and checked his ears prior to the surgery. He looked at me and smiled. He said, Mrs McCauley you can go home. Your son's hearing is perfect. He doesn't need my help today. Isaac went back to school for the afternoon session. The teacher asked why he was late. Isaac told them the whole story and thereafter his classmates nicknamed him, Holy Boy!

Brendan reminded Isaac of this healing and encouraged him to pray for me. Isaac was stirred up and shared this with me when he came home. I thought to myself, What am I doing feeling down? What use is that? I'd better hurry up and get healed so I can tell people Jesus is still healing today and is not just some ancient character in a dusty old book. The Bible says, Jesus is the same yesterday, today and forever. I remembered so many of the people we'd prayed for and seen healed over the years. Aidan Devine from Coleraine who drank Gramoxone weed killer and was given only days to live. Still alive and kicking after twenty years. Now married with a beautiful daughter. So many good things. So many people healed.

I shouted, I shall not die but I shall live, and I shall proclaim the works of the Lord.

Louder, I shall not die but I shall live, and I shall proclaim the works of the Lord.

Louder still, I shall not die but I shall live, and I shall proclaim the works of the Lord.

At that moment I chose life. I chose my healing so I could proclaim the works of the Lord. I broke the spirit of death over my life. The unbelief of the Christian youth leader and Isaac's friends stirred me on. So often the first response from Christians as regards healing is one of unbelief. Recently I left

Angela to school. I then went for a coffee in my favourite Ballynahinch café. It was buzzing with people. A well-dressed, middle-aged couple sat nearby. We struck up a conversation. I mentioned I'd been in Paris recently and this café reminded me of the small tables and limited space. They agreed. They'd also been to Paris. We laughed and talked. I told them my husband took me to Paris after I'd cancer.

I said, I'd colon cancer last year but now I'm healed.

The wife said, My husband has just been diagnosed with a tumour on his kidney. We're waiting for the next stage of treatment.

I said, Praise the Lord. He can be healed too.

The man said, Only if it's God's will. If God wants to heal me it's up to him. My heart went out to this poor man. He didn't know Jesus still heals. Probably never read Acts 10:38 where it says,

> *How God anointed Jesus of Nazareth with the Holy Spirit and power, and how he went around doing good and healing all who were under the power of the devil, because God was with him.*

Divine healing wasn't in his thinking. Just hoping for the best. Never been taught. Reminded me of Luke 5, where Jesus challenged the religious leaders,

Which is easier: to say, Your sins are forgiven, or to say, Get up and walk? But that you may know that the Son of Man has authority on earth to forgive sins... He said to the paralysed man, I tell you, get up, take your mat and go home. Immediately he stood up in front of them, took what he had been lying on and went home praising God.

Everyone was amazed and gave praise to God. They were filled with awe and said, We have seen remarkable things today.

How will people know unless someone tells them? Faith comes by hearing. So often fear prevents us from obtaining God's best. God help that lovely couple. They knew so little about God's promises concerning healing. I believe as we near the time of Jesus' return, the Church is not going to be clothed in filthy rags of fear and unbelief hiding out in the basement of some satanically bombed out building muttering ritual prayers and wringing her hands. Instead she will be a dazzling bride arrayed in garments of purity and power.

Ephesians 5 says, Christ loved the church and gave His life for it in order to present the church to Himself in all its beauty - pure and faultless, without spot or wrinkle or any other imperfection. Song of Solomon 6:10 says the Bride of Christ will be, She that looks forth as the morning, fair as the moon, clear as the sun, and terrible as an army with banners. Before Christ returns there'll be worldwide signs and wonders flowing through a Church more glorious and powerful than at her beginning.

At the end of May, eight weeks after our initial visit with the Indian doctor we drove through morning sunshine to meet another doctor who'd tell us the verdict. Had the cancer spread? How long would I live? We arrived early and were seen early. The doctor in his long white hair looked like Albert Einstein. He smiled. We smiled. It's not all bad, he said. There's no sign of cancer elsewhere in your body. Looks like its confined to your colon. He smiled. We smiled.

He showed us a photocopy of a scan and explained I'd a fourth degree tumour. We'd no idea what that meant. He said he'd have to cut away part of my lower rectum. Before this operation I'd be given five weeks of chemotherapy and radiotherapy in order to shrink the tumour. He'd operate six weeks after that. Like in Rachel McDowell's *Worm in the Apple* vision he'd cut away both good and infected parts of my rectum. He'd then create an opening in my side and I'd be given a bag to collect my waste. Hopefully this would be reversible. Any questions? We shook hands. He smiled.

Brendan and I went to celebrate. We sat outside at a restaurant in Lisburn Square and ate and drank and laughed and held hands in the warm sunshine. Glad to be alive and glad the cancer had not spread. Our children were relieved. The news was a huge reprieve for my daughter Shann who feared I'd drop dead any minute. My siblings, especially my sister Kathleen, were also relieved. Kathleen does voluntary work with a Marie Curie Cancer Care centre nearby. Kathleen regularly calls to see me after her weekly stint at the centre. She always brings me a parcel of soda and wheaten bread that reminds me of childhood days on the farm. I am touched by her kindness.

At this stage I felt built up because of God's daily blessings. Because of dreams and visions and prophecy. On the day we first discovered I'd cancer we called to tell our good friends John and Linda Thompson and tell them our bad news. They prayed and John prophesied the whole thing would be like a collection of days for me. And so it was. Every day God met me where I was. Someone would email me. Someone would phone me. Someone would talk to me. Something would happen. It was truly a collection of days. One day, our friend Kathleen McKee from Canada, emailed. God had told her I'd be 100% healed. Each day I listened to the healing CD.

Flowers were sent. Sweets were given. Letters arrived. Little tokens of affection. The body of Christ showing concern. Two large families from the local Catholic Church prayed and fasted for me. The nearby cross-denominational Saul Prayer Group prayed for me. One sunny day my sister Maureen brought me to a healing service in Clonard Monastery where I was anointed with oil. Brendan asked folk worldwide to pray. Our good friends Randy and Christine Emerson and the intercessors at Cloverdale Church in Surrey, Canada, regularly prayed for us. They constantly encouraged us by email. All over the world people I didn't even know were praying for me. My hairdresser Rosaleen prayed for me and kept me looking beautiful. My confidence in God returned. I felt better. I looked better. Some of my children bought me new clothes. I was being spoiled and indulged. I got beauty for ashes, the oil of joy for mourning and the garments of praise instead of the spirit of heaviness.

No *Angela's Ashes* for me.

A SPIRIT OF BITTERNESS

My maiden name was McEvoy. I'm from a family of ten children, two boys and eight girls. My cancer treatment was due to start on Monday. On Saturday we attended a McEvoy Gathering - an event that occurs every five years. It was a happy sunny day. Lovely to see all my children and grandchildren. Balloons, burgers and ice cream. Three legged races and tug of war. My smiling daughter Nora playing the violin.

Great to see my brothers and sisters and their children and children's children all looking so well. A few spouses were missing. Some had been taken by cancer. Brendan created a lovely Photobook of five generations of the McEvoy family for the occasion. He took more photographs on the day. Great pictures. Great memories. Everyone wished me well for my upcoming treatment.

On Sunday I was feeling apprehensive. Then Rosanne McDowell called and prayed with me. Next morning Hannah took me for my first treatment. Friends and family offered help with the driving. I was scheduled to have twenty-five sessions of radiotherapy over a five-week period. Each day I'd get an eighty-second blast into my back. I'd also to take two tablets of chemotherapy, one in the morning, one in the evening.

I was shaken after the first session. I came home, felt down and lay down. I thought, This is going to kill me. That night Isaac had a dream. In his dream he saw a piece of paper. On it was written, The blood is not getting to the tumour. Isaac didn't know whether this was good or bad. In the dream he passed this information on to his sister Dr. Mary. Mary said, Praise God. This is excellent news. It means the cancer is being starved of blood. The cancer is dying. In the dream they came to see me. They told me about the blood not getting to the cancer. I said, I already know but I'm waiting for the doctors to find it out. In the end the doctors will tell me the cancer is gone!

Next morning Isaac shared his dream and I was very encouraged. I'd already sensed the blood was not getting to the tumour. From the Bible I know the life is in the blood. The tumour was being denied life so I knew it must die. This dream strengthened me. On the second morning of my treatment I went off to the hospital full of hope and joy.

Next day my daughter Ruth came home from Geneva. She expected me to be lying sick in bed. Instead I was up and about. Ruth and Hannah took me to my next treatment. We arranged to meet up with my daughter Nora for lunch. It was the week of graduations at Queens University Belfast. The streets were full of advertisements for special graduation meals. I said to my girls, For years now I've been going to my children's graduations but today prophetically I'm going to celebrate my own graduation from cancer. Pick the best restaurant! Nora suggested *Cayenne* owned by celebrity chef Paul Rankin. The food was beautiful. I had lamb. I also remembered another lamb who gave his life for me and by whose stripes I am healed and I gave thanks. It was a lovely graduation lunch with my daughters. I'll never forget it.

Ruth then took me downtown and bought me a fashionable dress and cardigan. I came home and threw out old dark dresses I'd had for years. I thought to myself, The Lord will turn my mourning into dancing. From then on I only wore colourful dresses to my treatments.

Four days into the treatment and I was in a foul mood. My daughter Hannah had met a friend who'd recently attempted suicide. Hannah told her friend I had cancer. She also mentioned I'd kept quiet about the bleeding. The friend said the one thing they'd learned from their suicide attempt was never ever to keep things to oneself. They said there was always someone willing to listen, someone willing to help. The friend told Hannah to tell me never to keep things hidden again. After Hannah shared this I became annoyed. I'd been bleeding from my back passage for nearly three years and I hadn't felt free to share it with anyone. After Hannah left I was distressed.

Then Brendan waltzed in, Hello Love. How you doing?

Don't how you doing me!

He said, Hot and mad like a bee in a bird's beak?

I shared my upset. I started shouting, You're my husband. Get me help. Get me some help.

Brendan decided he needed some space. He went to the local supermarket muttering, Dog food, doghouse. Dog food, doghouse. Dog food, doghouse.

At the store he bumped into our friend Rosanne. She too needed some space from her spouse. Roseanne said her husband Laurence had called at our home on Sunday to pray for me but no one was in. Brendan suggested Rosanne should immediately get back into unity with Laurence and the pair of them should come and pray for me immediately. We're in the middle of a divine appointment, he said. Now is the hour.

Brendan arrived home looking happy as a sandboy. He said, Don't worry Angela. Help is on its way. Fifteen spirit of bitterness

minutes later Laurence and Rosanne arrived. They started praying. Laurence discerned a spirit of bitterness. His daughter Rachel who had the *Apple and Worm* vision had also sensed the worm represented a spirit of bitterness. I believe bitterness was the source of my cancer, the fox in the bowels of my house. Hebrews 12 warns,

> *Therefore lift your drooping hands and strengthen your weak knees, and make straight paths for your feet, so that what is lame may not be put out of joint but rather be healed. Strive for peace with everyone, and for the holiness without which no one will see the Lord. See to it that no one fails to obtain the grace of God; that no root of bitterness springs up and causes trouble, and by it many become defiled;*

A root of bitterness is not easily discovered. Like a fox in the bowels of a house it does its insidious work deep in the marrow of one's soul. Only after it metastasises do symptoms surface in bitter words, bitter thoughts and bitter deeds. Bitterness can affect us all. Children bitter towards parents. Parents bitter toward children. The divorced and their children get bitter. Siblings get bitter over parental affection and inheritances. How much bitterness caused by the reading of a will?

When bitterness spreads its tentacles many become defiled. Could that explain some of my own children's rebellion? Do we really reap what we sow? The doctors wanted to cut the cancer from my body but thankfully Jesus was using the fiery furnace to remove bitterness from my spirit. Years ago I had a dream in which a strongman of rejection was pressing me against a wall. In the dream Brendan came and chased that spirit away. Sometime later Brendan actually cast that demon from me. Rejection had troubled me all my life now thankfully it was gone. Rebellion also had gone and now a strongman of bitterness had been cast out. The fiery furnace was doing its work burning the cords that bound me.

1 John 1:9 says, If we confess our sins, he is faithful and just to forgive us our sins, and to cleanse us from all unrighteousness. I wanted rid of all bitterness. I was truly grateful help had arrived in the form of Laurence and Rosanne. The body of Christ was working to help and to heal. Like the suicidal person I hadn't previously asked for help. But the suicidal person was right. If we need help we should ask for it. Jesus would agree, Ask and you shall receive.

Although I'd been bleeding for three years it stopped within a week of me telling Brendan. My appetite also returned. Only one symptom remained. I'd get cold and sore in my lower body if I went outside. After Laurence and Rosanne prayed I knew in my heart I was healed. Afterwards I could go out and about without any further feelings of coldness or soreness.

In fact I was feeling so well that four days later at my

weekly review I told the doctor I wanted to stop all treatment. I said God had healed me. I told the doctor he could do a test to prove it. Brendan was insistent I should have proof my cancer was gone before I stopped all treatment. In Matthew 8 Jesus told the leper to go and show himself to the priest so the priest could verify the healing and the leper could be restored to the community. Getting proof from the doctor today is much like going to the priest in those days. Brendan said if the doctor verified there was no sign of cancer in my body then he would allow me to stop. He said he wasn't willing to play games with my life. He loved me and he wanted the best for me. He said he had a responsibility to me, to my children and to my grandchildren.

The doctor said, Mrs McCauley I've worked with colon cancer patients for over thirty years. In all that time there has only ever been one person who didn't need an operation.

I thought, I am number two!

He said, Mrs McCauley you must continue with the treatment.

I backed down believing Brendan would want me to do so.

On Wednesday 14th July Brendan woke up and said he'd just had a dream in which he was informed two women were healed of cancer in the lower parts of their body.

I believed one of those women was me. An hour later I tried to phone someone and I got Judy McGookin from Coleraine instead. No idea how it happened. Judy said she was just that minute thinking of me. In fact she was going to fast for me that day. She said she was fasting for two women who were battling cancer, me and another lady in England. I thought this is the fulfilment of Brendan's dream. A while later I rang another friend Stephanie Quigley also of Coleraine and told her I believed I was healed. She said she'd fast for me that day as well. So two holy women were fasting for me. It must have been God.

Next day at my weekly review the young doctor asked how I was feeling. I told him I was feeling good. So good in fact that I wanted to stop the treatment. I truly believed I was healed. I'd no symptoms or any ill effects from the radiotherapy. I was even more convinced I was healed than when I'd talked to the previous doctor.

He said, Mrs McCauley it's unheard of that you should stop your treatment at this stage. You must finish the course.

I said, But I'm healed.

He was perplexed. He said, Mrs McCauley if we do a scan and it's found you still have cancer will you continue with the treatment?

I said, If the cancer is still there I'll continue with the

treatment.

He said, Mrs McCauley I'll be the first to give you a big hug if we discover the tumour is gone. He went and talked to a radiographer who agreed to do a scan. This was Thursday. Next day I didn't go for my scheduled treatment.

Brendan was very unhappy when he found out. His face looked like a plateful of mortal sins. I told him I was healed. Wasn't that what he wanted? Didn't he take me to Zakynthos to build up my faith when I was a scared little hedgehog? Didn't he pray for me day and night? Could he not understand I was healed?

Brendan said he thought the fiery furnace was still in operation. He said he didn't think Shadrach, Meshach and Abednego could just walk out of the fiery furnace whenever they wanted. There was a process to it all. He talked about testing revelation, about weighing things up and walking humbly before God. He quoted Colossians 3:15, Let the peace of Christ rule in your hearts, since as members of one body you were called to peace. And be thankful. He said, Angela I don't have any peace in my heart you should stop your treatment at this point. I honestly don't feel the timing is right. I sense there is still some fiery furnace work to be done.

We both wanted to be led by the Holy Spirit. Both wanted to do the right thing. Dreams, prophetic words and supernatural events concerning my healing were happening almost daily. It was hard to balance things. Working with the doctors. Working with my husband. Working with the Lord. Working with other people. I remembered when I'd a badly broken knee some years earlier. An English prophetess Rosemary Andrews prophesied from a stage in a hotel in Bray, Co. Wicklow that God was healing me. At that point against all the advice of Brendan and the doctors I chose to discard my crutches and walk. I also remembered when I was a child I had rheumatic fever. Afterwards the doctors advised I should only ever have one child because my heart was in such a poor condition. They kept me in hospital for a month before the birth of my first baby.

I've absolutely nothing whatsoever against the medical profession. After all I have two nurses and one doctor amongst my children so far. It's just that doctors haven't always given me great advice or great respect over the years. In fact a few years ago Hannah helped me to get all my medical notes as regards my fourteen pregnancies due to a change in some disclosure of information act. I discovered one Catholic doctor had written to his colleague after I had six children. He wrote, This unfortunate woman is pregnant again. I was pregnant with Ruth, a brilliant girl, who went on to study law in Cambridge. Seems that Catholic doctor neither listened to the Pope nor read his Bible.

But when I saw how upset Brendan was as regards my decision to stop the treatment I reassessed the situation. So that night before we went to sleep I told him I would continue the treatment on one condition.

I said, If you want me to continue the treatment then you must come with me each day. You were at the birth of all fourteen of our children. Be with me now. I need your support.

He said, It's a deal. Let's kiss on it.

PRETTY WOMAN

One morning I awakened with a yearning for fresh vegetable soup. Although it was summer my body needed the nutrients. I called my son Isaac and gave him precise instructions of what to do. My daughter Nora had put up a work rota for David, Jacob, Isaac, Abraham and Angela but it definitely wasn't working. Lazy, hazy, crazy days of summer. I called Isaac because he was the most cooperative one.

I said, Go down to Hanlons and buy fresh onions, garlic, carrots, parsnips, celery, parsley, leeks and a packet of chicken stock cubes. Then come home immediately and make the soup. Brendan noticed Isaac wasn't really paying attention. He suggested Isaac get a pen and paper and write down my instructions. After some huffing and puffing Isaiah found pen and paper. I told him if he couldn't find any of the items to go up to the counter and ask an assistant for help.

Isaac ran down to the shop and returned surprisingly quickly. I asked him if he'd any problems getting the stuff. He said, No. I asked to see the vegetables. I wanted to smell their lovely earthiness. Isaac produced a tin of vegetable soup. Soon Brendan arrived notified by the raised female voice in the kitchen. He discovered Isaac had run down to Hanlons and asked the pretty female assistant for a tin of vegetable soup. Brendan asked to see Isaac's list. Isaac produced a crumpled bit of paper with the words onions, carrots and leeks on it.

Brendan again told Isaac to listen to me and take a proper list this time. Isaac went back to the shop picked the vegetables and went to the counter to pay.

The pretty female assistant asked, Tin of soup no good?

Isaac said, No.

Was it for your Mammy?

Isaac blushed.

Why does your Mammy want soup in the middle of summer?

Isaac wished he'd obtained the correct vegetables in

one flesh

the first place. Eventually I got the lovely fresh soup and Isaac learned a lesson. David, Jacob, Abraham and Angela still fast asleep learned nothing. Brendan put his arm around Isaac. He said, Don't worry son. I wonder just how often God gives us specific instructions through dreams, visions, prophecies and so on and we end up taking shortcuts and thinking we're clever people? Maybe God's like your Mom. He knows what he wants and he'll hold out for it. Perhaps he really does want his kingdom to come on earth in his way. What do you think?

Brendan accompanied me for the remaining twelve days of treatment. I felt secure with him. I didn't have to put on a brave face with Brendan. Also there's always something happening with Brendan. He started bringing books in and leaving them for patients in a little space provided for that purpose.

He started getting two paper cups of coffee and a large sausage roll from the hospital café and bringing them into the treatment room. He'd break the sausage roll in half and give me the big half. Then we'd imagine we were picnicking on Kalamaki beach in Zakynthos or some bistro in Paris. Laughing and joking like young lovers. When we'd come home from the treatment Brendan would often be exhausted like he was helping to carry the burden. I found this beneficial. The Scriptures say married people are one flesh. I liked it that Brendan was also going through the fiery trail with me.

One Saturday I had a very strange experience. I experienced one full day of sickness. It felt as if God took his hand of protection off me to show just how bad things could have been. I was very nauseous. Dry retching. Terrible pains in my body. In the middle of me being sick my friend Linda Thompson phoned. God had put it on her heart to pray for me and she reacted immediately. Her timing encouraged me.

That evening Brendan's niece, Louise, rang. She said God had told her I was under his divine protection and I should give thanks for what he'd done for me. She said she'd a dream in which I was visiting Brendan's mother with my family and I was looking so well. Brendan's brother John, Louise's dad, was also there. In the dream I told everyone I had good news to tell them. Louise also said God told her he was the one who'd taught me how to pray. She felt I should thank God for his daily protection.

Louise's words were so appropriate on my day of sickness. It felt as if just for one day God was showing me what the effects of the chemotherapy and radiotherapy could have been like. Afterwards I had no more sickness. Praise God for his hedge of protection around me as in Job 1:10, Have you not put a hedge around him and his household and everything he has? You have blessed the work of his hands, so that his flocks and herds are spread throughout the land.

One day young Angela had an appointment with her

orthodontist in Bangor at 9.30 in the morning. We planned to take her there and then drive on to Belfast for my session. I found it tough getting out of bed so we were already behind time before we hit bad traffic. We arrived 20 minutes late. Brendan dropped us off and went to park. I apologised to a stony faced receptionist. She said, I don't think you can be seen today. You'll need to come back in a couple of months. That's the earliest available appointment.

I said, We've travelled a long distance in bad traffic. My daughter is due to have her braces removed today. I don't think she can wait two more months.

Perhaps we'll wait and see if she still can be seen..

She said, Please yourself but you won't be seen today.

Brendan arrived in. He was carrying three cups of coffee and three small sausage rolls. He said, You're both looking down-in-the-mouth. What's up? He handed me a present. I unwrapped it and started laughing. The receptionists glared at us. His present was a wooden wall plaque. It had a small nighttime window with a *No Vacancies* sign hanging on it. The main part of the plaque said,

My Husband said he needed more space.

So I locked him outside.

I was laughing and giggling like a schoolgirl because only a few days earlier Brendan had been complaining about needing more space. As I munched on my sausage roll he asked, What's the story Morning Glory? I explained my talk with Miss Frosty.

He said, Do you want me to deal with it?

That's why you're here.

I secretly hoped Brendan would give the receptionist a good telling off. I felt she deserved it. But he was gracious. He went in to another room where he wouldn't embarrass anyone. I could still see him through a hatch. Miss Frosty busied herself at a computer. Brendan spoke to her colleague. He said, I wonder can you help me? My wife Angela is in her final stages of cancer treatment. It's has been a very bad morning. Difficult for her to get out of bed. I rushed here as best I could but we hit bad traffic. I don't know if my daughter can wait a couple of months to have her braces off. We also have an appointment in the cancer ward later this morning. I'm trying to do my best but I really don't know what to do now. I'll do whatever you think best. Can you help me please?

Within minutes Angela's braces had been removed and we were on our way rejoicing. The orthodontist told Angela to convey her best wishes to me. Now we had time to spare before my appointment. We decided to call and see our friends Dr Bob & Louise Caswell now in their late eighties. We chatted and remembered old times. We talked about them praying with nuns when the Charismatic wave hit Ireland in the 1970s and how radical a thing that was then. They have been very faithful intercessors over many years. As we left after tea and a time of prayer I thought of Ecclesiastes 3,

> *There is a time for everything,*
> *And a season for every activity under heaven:*
> *A time to be born and a time to die,*
> *A time to plant and a time to uproot,*
> *A time to kill and a time to heal,*

This was my time to heal. Then suddenly it was my final day in the fiery furnace. Young Angela accompanied Brendan and me. Brendan and Angela went for the coffee and sausage rolls and I found a seat. Then I went to the toilet. When I came out Brendan was standing looking confused.

I said, What's the matter?

He said, I thought I'd lost you.

I'd only taken one bite out of my big half of the sausage roll when I was quickly ushered in for my last blast. I warned Brendan, Please don't eat my sausage roll. I was in and out in a few minutes. As I walked back to my snack I heard a loud banging noise like someone hammering tin. Then music. Then Roy Orbison's three-octave operatic voice,

> *Pretty woman, walking down the street*
> *Pretty woman, the kind I like to meet*
> *Pretty woman*
> *I don't believe you, you're not the truth*
> *No one could look as good as you*
> *Mercy*

Suddenly every head turned in my direction. They were all looking at me. Brendan was holding a Portable iPod Speaker Dock. Then my daughters Nora and Mary came to me in a bustle of balloons and laughter and presented me with large bouquets of flowers. I was so overcome I nearly forgot about my sausage roll. Nurses and radiotherapists popped out of rooms to see this little moment of joy in the cancer ward.

The fiery furnace door popped open and all the people began to applaud. I flushed bright red.

Brendan took me in his arms. He said, Well done!

INTO THE MARVELLOUS

The stress was telling on Brendan. Apart from caring for me he regularly visited his mom whose condition was life threatening. Our friends Stephen and Judy McGookin were holidaying in Donegal. I asked could we join them for a couple of days. The weather was glorious. Best two days in a hundred years. The views and beaches spectacular. Halcyon days.

Second morning Brendan and I walked an empty beach. Same beach we'd walked with our young family over twenty years before. I'd forgotten how beautiful it all was. Depression darkens beauty. In my memory I could still see the children, canoeing and swimming and squealing with laughter. Still see the shells falling out of their hands as they followed each other back up the hill.

Brendan spied something shiny in the sand. Turned out to be a child's kite with a smiley face. He teased out the coloured tail and then freed bits and pieces of the kite. It was badly tangled and mangled encrusted with old sinewy and new blubbery seaweed. Looked like a lost cause but Brendan took pity on it. For the next hour with the sun on our backs we sat on a rock swinging our legs. I watched Brendan as he patiently unravelled the tattered mess. When it was finally straightened out he discovered one of the crosspieces was missing.

He scanned the beach for an answer. He spliced two pieces of dried weed and used that for the missing support and hey presto the whole thing went sky high. Up into the marvellous morning. Its little smiley face weaving and bobbing in the sunshine. My heart turned. He handed me the string and when I took the tug my youth was restored.

I've seen advertisements claiming I could look up to ten years younger in four weeks if I'd use a certain anti-wrinkle cream. But when Brendan handed me that kite I lost fifty years in five seconds. I was a young girl again on a Saturday night in Newcastle. Make mine a 99! I walked barefoot for over an hour playing with my newfound friend newly restored to its proper place. Then I lay on my back in the warm sand and watched that happy smiley face for such a long time. Brendan sat watching me.

Judy loves the waves. That evening she and Brendan went body boarding at a nearby beach. Big white waves and a big red sun. Stephen and I taking pictures on our mobiles. Brendan has always been good in the water. Taught all our children to swim. And now he was swimming again like a strong man in the full vigour of youth. Judy and Brendan catching waves in a setting sun, two carers all at sea without a care in the world.

Then August and exam results. Everyone did well. All back on track after last year's stumbling. Now five children at University. Only two at home. We've become a normal nuclear family. How lonely it is. Brendan's mom's health rallied and she went back to live in her own home.

Six weeks after my last treatment I was called in for an appointment prior to the operation. The doctors still planned to remove part of my colon and insert a stoma in my side to collect my waste. I remembered Jesus was pierced for my transgressions. On the cross his side was sliced open. I believed my side would remain intact. Brendan came with me. His position was still, Go show yourself to the priest. He said, Angela, if a scan confirms there's no tumour in your body then I won't force you to have an operation. There's absolutely nothing wrong with proof. I only want the best for you.

Life had been busy since my last treatment. We'd hosted a prophetic weekend conference in Drumalis Retreat Centre in Larne. We'd been to Kerry, Donegal and Greece. My strength was coming back. I was in good form, telling everyone I was healed. This doctor at the appointment was new to us. He started speaking about my sister having cancer and how it would be advisable for me to have a colonoscopy in order to make sure everything was okay. Brendan stopped him at this point. He said, Doctor, are you're sure you've got the right person? Turned out he'd been given the wrong notes. He sent for mine but they never turned up.

He improvised, What exactly is your situation Mrs. McCauley?

I said, I've been through five weeks of radiotherapy and chemotherapy. Now God has healed me.

The doctor looked at Brendan.

Brendan smiled.

He said, Mrs McCauley the treatment was not meant to cure you. Its purpose was to shrink the tumour. You must have the operation.

I said, Jesus has healed me. I don't need an operation.

He went next door to talk to his colleague. He returned sticking to his guns. He said, Mrs McCauley you must have this operation.

I said, No thank you doctor. I'm healed. We left.

The doctors were now in a tizzy. My answer phone full of messages. They'd had a cancellation. The main doctor wanted to do a colonoscopy on me. Monday at nine o clock in the morning. Brendan and I were scheduled to fly to Canada on Friday.

The pleasant secretary asked, Can you make it okay?

Yes I'll be there.

The cherry trees were now ablaze with autumn glory. I'd been nervous when I first came there in springtime but now God had healed me I was excited. Glad of the chance to show myself to the priest.

A nurse met me. I said, Jesus has healed me.

She said, That's good.

I told the doctor I was healed.

He nodded and smiled.

The camera was inserted. I could see live pictures of my colon on the screen. The doctor probed around with the camera. Nurses looked on. He seemed surprised. After a while he pointed to an area as pink and healthy as a baby's cheek. He said, That's where the tumour was.

I nodded and smiled.

I said, That's good.

A nurse said, Look what we're doing now. We are working miracles.

I was laughing for joy, saying, Praise the Lord.

The doctor took biopsies from the place where the tumour had been. The atmosphere in the room was festive. When Brendan was allowed in he asked, What's happening? Circus come to town?

I told him the good news.

He said, Well done!

I said, That's the fifteenth time you've told me that.

He kissed me.

The doctor showed Brendan and me some scans and discussed the results. He said, There is no sign whatsoever of the cancer. This is the best possible result you could have hoped for.

As good as it gets, said Brendan.

The doctor immediately wrote a letter. He gave me a copy before I left. It said,

Dear Doctor,

Angela McCauley underwent long course chemo-radiotherapy for adenoccarcinoma of the rectum and rectosigmoid junction. Mrs. McCauley attended this morning for assessment of the rectal tumour. The flexible sigmoidoscopy was performed without sedation. Mrs. McCauley's bowel was well prepared and a view to the splendid flexure was obtained. The rectum was entirely clear. At the rectosigmoid junction and extending for two to three centimetres was a short segment of mucosal inflammation consistent with the radiotherapy. There was no obvious tumour, but the mucosal was biopsied at this site. I have recommended continuing with the original plan of anterior reaction although I know Mrs. McCauley has decided against this. Nevertheless I have suggested a second opinion with my colleague.

Yours sincerely.

I started calling this letter, my certificate. It took a while between my graduation dinner in Belfast and receiving my certificate but in the end I got it. Some people find divine healing difficult to take. They want proof. The doctor in his letter still suggested I should continue with the original plan but what else is a doctor going to recommend?

Next day I saw the doctor's colleague for a second opinion. I told him God had healed me. He kept looking at a screen. He said, Mrs. McCauley you don't understand. It may seem to you the tumour has gone. But believe me tumours don't just disappear. This is a Grade 4 tumour - T4 N1 MO. It's as big as an orange and it's broken the wall.

I said, Thank you Doctor. From your point of view you feel I still need an operation to be safe. But from my point of view I believe God has removed the tumour. And if God has done it then he's done a good job. There will be no cancer whatsoever in my body. I'm more than willing to take a CAT scan to prove it.

A couple of weeks later, after Canada, I got the biopsy results. They were all clear. I then had the CAT scan. A couple of weeks after that the results came back saying there was no sign of cancer in my body. God had indeed done a good job.

In May my daughter Ruth and her husband Stuart sent me a small olive tree for my birthday. I put into the conservatory and promptly neglected it. Eventually Brendan broke a number of branches off to test for life. It was as dead as doornails. He kept the pot and chucked the dead tree on to the compost heap. What would we tell Ruth? Months later Brendan called me into the garden. He said, You won't believe this.

There lying on the compost heap was my neglected olive tree. I moved closer. I could hardly believe my eyes. My dead olive tree had sprouted new leaves. We repotted it and put it in pride of place at our front door where it now stands speaking to all who have eyes to see and ears to hear.

As Brendan might say, If this was a dream what would it mean?

Contact details:

Mrs Angela McCauley
PO Box 38
Downpatrick
County Down
Northern Ireland
BT30 6YH

email address: prayingangela@hotmail.com

website: www.threefoldcord.info

We appreciate hearing from you!